IGNASI DE SOLÀ-M

JUJO

JUJOL

Photographs:
MELBA LEVIC

Ediciones Polígrafa

Both the publishers and the author would like
to express their gratitude to the directors of
the Jujol Archives, Quaderns d'Arquitectura,
Escola Tècnica Superior d'Arquitectura de
Barcelona and the Arxiu de la Catedral
de Ciutat de Mallorca for their kind
permission to reproduce graphic documents
belonging to them.

© Photographs: Melba Levick
Graphic design: M. Antònia Miserachs
Translated by:
Jennifer Jackson and Kerstin Engström

I.S.B.N. 84-343-0628-X
D. L.: B. 37.958 - 1990 (Printed in Spain)

Color separation: Reprocolor Llovet, S. A.
Printed by La Polígrafa, S. A.
Parets del Vallès (Barcelona)

Final year project. Thermal Bath Building, 1905 (ETSAB Archive).

Lluís Casals

Josep M.ª Jujol

It is usual practice to devote monographic studies to great figures, to outstanding architectural works, and to personalities whose influence at a particular moment has characterized the work of succeeding generations.

This book, however, is an exception to the rule. Josep M.ª Jujol is an architect as unique as he is little known. Hardly any recent articles and catalogs have even begun to consider him, forty years after his death, and seventy or eighty years after the construction of his most representative buildings.

Now, however, at the end of the century, when it has become impossible to write one single all-embracing history of modern architecture, the figure of the architect from Tarragona seems to grow by the moment. Despite his having been forgotten and put to one side of the linear history of the different trends which have succeeded each other throughout our century, this is a set of works which contains lessons and suggestions which are fascinating from the point of view not only of their sheer vitality and the honesty of their realization, but also because of the light they shed on our present situation.

While Jujol is no antecedent to one of the latest trends, there is in the personal isolation of his work a clear reference to the perplexities that run through the art of our time.

1. Formative Years

Josep M.ª Jujol Gibert was born in Tarragona on 16 September 1879 in the primary-school building in which the family lived and where his father worked as a teacher. He was to live in that city for the first nine years of his life, in a modest but cultivated environment in which curiosity about both nature and culture would be on a par with a religious education, which occupied a central place in all spheres of the family's life.

In 1888, due to a change in the professional destiny of his father, the family moved to what was then the town of Gràcia, which shortly afterwards would be annexed to the city of Barcelona.

Jujol first attended a state school, and later the Institut de Batxillerat, where he completed his studies brilliantly in 1896. It was in the autumn of this same year that he began his university education, first in the Faculty of Science and later, as from 1901-1902, in the School of Architecture of Barcelona.

Jujol was to graduate in 1906, having attended class regularly. Outstanding amongst his fellow students and friends who graduated in the same year were the future architects Josep M.ª Pericas and Rafael Masó i Valentí.

During those years the atmosphere at the Barcelona School of Architecture was determined by the figure of its undisputed director, Lluís Domènech i Montaner. The whole of the far-reaching artistic and architectural *modernista* movement, which began at least in 1888 and progressed well into the second decade of the twentieth century, revolved without doubt around the teachings of two great contemporary architects: Lluís Domènech i Montaner (1850-1923) and Antoni Gaudí (1852-1926).

However, whereas the first was a key figure in the academic world, so that his message was transmitted from the classroom, through publications and research activity, and also through the extent of his constructed work, in the case of Gaudí his teaching was exactly the opposite, being on a personal level, carried out independently from academic structure, and based on reflections arising from having lived and experienced the problems posed by each of his works.

The colossal weight of these two figures is the best point of reference from which to see and appreciate the coordinating lines of the formative years of Jujol and the architects of his generation.

The generation that followed that of the disciples and immediate collaborators of these two great personalities (Gallissà, Font i Gumà, Granell, Puig i Cadafalch, Rubió i Bellver, Moncunill, etc.) had a different attitude to the *modernista* environment.

On the one hand, the weight of these great figures was vouched for both by the splendour of their works and the loyalty of their followers. On the other, there emerged an alternative between the eclectic rationality of the balanced and brilliant Domènech line and the figurative and constructive radicalness of the Gaudí circle. Finally there was the internationalization of the end-of-century phenomenon with the increasingly closer influence of parallel movements which in France *(Art Nouveau)*, in Germany *(Jugendstil)*, in Holland *(Wendingen)* or in Austria *(Sezession)* denoted aspects similar to one and the same historical crisis, while also being responses peculiar to each individual situation.

Although Jujol only once traveled out of his country, and that was already in the twenties, it is certain that contextually he could not have been ignorant of the parallel currents which in those years ran through the classrooms of the Barcelona School of Architecture. The true influence of central Europe on Jujol's friends — Massó, Pericas, Goday and Jeroni Martorell — gives us sufficient authority to state both that Jujol was no stranger to these, and that curiosity concerning the work of Olbrich, Makintosh or Berlague must have been a constant source of discussion among that last generation of *modernista* architects. In this, as in many other things, Jujol was to show his ability for placing himself at the crossroads of different attitudes and trends, making of them a very personalized synthesis which at all times placed him at a far remove from easy subscription to stereotyped tendencies.

It is his fabulous capacity as a painter and draftsman that above all characterizes his formative years. A good student in the discipline of the sciences, Jujol was already in his student years an exceptional draftsman.

There is in this field of the plastic arts a moment of dissolution of the *modernista* iconography, which in the first decade of the century is characterized by the construction of forms through the use of a luxurious interplay of colors in their pure state. In the paintings of Lluís Masriera, classicist mythology is dissolved by color in the same way that the landscape is dissolved in the great oil paintings of Joaquim Mir or Hermen Anglada Camarasa. It is also the time of post-Cézannian color experiments carried out in Barcelona by Picasso and his friend Isidre Nonell. In that atmosphere of graphic experimentation which existed in Barcelona at the turn of the century, the diffusion of a whole new school of graphics holds a key place. Lluís Bagaria, Xavier Gosé and Miquel Utrillo reveal the end-of-century taste for infinite lines, the play of free areas of color on the paper, and the vivid contrast between colors.

It is in the light of these plastic experiments that we can understand the transference of pictorial sensitivity to the field of architecture in a case as clear as that of Jujol. Throughout his life he was to be a transitory artist dividing his time between architecture, sculpture, the decorative arts and drawing, reaching the point of being appointed lecturer not only in the School of Architecture, but also in the School of Arts and Crafts at the Industrial University. His work specifically as an architect and designer can be viewed not only from the standpoint of his stature as a draftsman, but also from his having moved in a direction parallel to that of contemporary plastic artists, in which of course he stood well aloof from the academic drawing style then employed by the majority of Barcelona architects.

If we examine Jujol's student projects, both those kept in the archives of the School of Architecture and by the Jujol family, we shall observe the convergence of opposing influences.

While the project for a Historical Archive of Catalunya (1904) responds to the typical Domènech way of teaching, on the other hand the project for the Votive Church dedicated to Santa Eulàlia (1905) is a first example of Gaudian issue of the surpassing of the traditional Gothic building with special attention being paid to the composition of the chapel of the central ground plan. His graduation project, on the other hand, is the monumental Thermal Baths building (1906), which bears witness to another type of sensitivity and interest. Firstly, the technique of representation is more mature, personalized and consequently freer. Secondly, it is his personal approach to a classical theme but with an understanding of classical thermal architecture which is more evocative of the sublime eighteenth-century style than the rigors of the *Beaux-arts* tradition. This project that Jujol realizes at the time of his early collaboration with Gaudí points towards a tendency that will always be present in his work: the treatment of form through the use of color, and even in a building as tectonically solid as the project for the Thermal Baths, there appears to be a play of light and shade enhanced by the skilful use of water-color. The talent of craftsman and colorist so often praised in Jujol is the not simple virtuosity of a neutral technique of representation, but a vehicle through which architecture can be imagined in color, the light and the arabesque of the lines that constitute — as in the painting of Miró or in the graphics of Picasso — an approach to architecture which is peculiar to and unmistakably that of Jujol.

But Jujol's training was not the exclusive product of his studies in the School of Architecture, for it is quite possible that his apprenticeship with some architects in whose studios the young student learned and collaborated was of far greater importance.

The first architects' studio in which he combined his hours of university study with the practice of design was in that of Antoni M.ª Gallissà. Between 1901 and 1903 he collaborated with this follower of Domènech, a delicate and attentive cultivator of the smallest details. Here Jujol freely designed for him sgraffiti, ceramics and ironwork. Jujol's intervention, which on occasions is easily recognizable from the personality of his characteristic features and his style of calligraphy, can be detected in some the last works of his ill-fated maestro, who died in 1903.

Jujol also worked for a short time with another prestigious architect, Josep Font i Gumà, with whom he collaborated on the design of an altar, now no longer existing, for the church of Santa Maria del Mar, and also on alterations to the Barcelona Athenaeum situated in Carrer Canuda.

But the most decisive collaboration in Jujol's formative years as an architect was with Antoni Gaudí. This was to mark him with an indelible stamp, to the point where some authors do not consider Jujol to be anything more than a simple follower of Gaudí. The truth, however, seems to be rather more complex, in a relationship which is, in a sense, that of maestro and disciple, but which from another point of view supposes a kind of collaboration in which the specific contribution of Jujol can be clearly distinguished from the work of a mere executor of his patron's ideas.

Jujol's collaboration with Gaudí began possibly at the beginning of 1906, arising from his contact with Dr. Santaló as a result of work on the Barcelona Athenaeum. With the architect of the Sagrada Família Jujol was to maintain a clear relation of disciple and executor of his maestro's instructions; even so, and thanks to his talent, he was progressively allowed greater creative freedom.

Relations between Jujol and Gaudí remained stable for four or five years: a day-to-day collaboration which gradually changed into a relationship that allowed our architect to take on his own commissions, some even given by Gaudí himself or by people associated with him.

This is characteristic of the type of collaboration that Gaudí's disciples maintained with their maestro: familiarizing themselves with his explanations; carrying out specific works; assisting him more permanently in some works; accompanying him on his visits to the building sites or in work with the suppliers of material; this was almost always the type of relationship established by Gaudí with the architects of his circle, who on many occasions considered themselves rewarded above all by the experimental excitement which reigned in his studio and by the participation in architectural works which were always conceived as a kind of collective enterprise.

Gaudí's historians have often tended to undervalue the importance of Jujol's contributions to his work between 1905 and 1912, as if this contribution detracts from the unquestionable division of roles between maestro and disciple. But the history of architecture is full of examples of collaborations by young artists in the work of their seniors and whose intervention is recognizable without being undermined by the importance of the principal architect. Wright with Sullivan, Mies van der Rohe with Behrens, are both clear examples of a productive relationship in which the stimulation of the maestro does not eclipse the genius of the young disciple at the moment of his creative incorporation in the projects of the former.

Jujol's intervention in the work of Gaudí is in some cases easy to identify. In a sense he contributed to the experimental rationalism of Gaudí with his decorative and pictorial imagination, producing even the most enchanting colorist and freely ornamental period of Gaudí's production.

Probably Jujol's first important participation in a building by Gaudí is his work on Casa Batlló, where we know that the colored decoration of the façade, some details of ironwork and pictorial motifs of some of the rooms on the first floor were carried out with great personal freedom. The explosion of areas of color extending like a skin sliding over a relatively static composition of hollows on the façade denotes a way of working that is typical of Jujol: the superimposing of architectural elements without excessive concern about the unity between the previous structure and the decorative form.

Project for the decoration of the Festes de la Mercè in the Carrer de Ferran, Barcelona, 1908 (Jujol Archive).

Canopy for the new high altar in the
Cathedral of the city of Mallorca, 1910
(Archive of the Cathedral, City of
Mallorca).

set on the façade of undulating stone,
grew and took shape in his hands.

Jujol was also a major protagonist
in the construction of certain details
of Park Güell. Gaudí entrusted to his
disciple the execution of at least two
fundamental decorative elements, one
being the finishing of the interiors
of the semi-spherical domes which
would cover the hypostyle room in
the center of the park; the other was
the positioning and finishing of the
seat covered in ceramics that forms
the limits of the large upper plaza
which is on top of the previously
mentioned hypostyle room. In the
circles of the hypostyle room Jujol
created the famous circular rosettes
made from discarded ceramic and
glass. Broken fragments of bottles,
plates, china and ceramic, iron strips.
A brilliant setting made of these
worthless remains is transformed into
a vaguely heraldic design evocative of
fantastic figures and animals, creating
a multicolored counterpoint to the
spherical surface of the interior of the
domes covered in white ceramic.

As was happening in other parts of
Europe (Vienna, Munich, Brussels)
here too there was a reinterpretation
of the Byzantine universe as a meeting
point between classical objectivity and
the fantasy of oriental architects.

In the bench that crowns the upper
plaza, the interplay of positioning
achieved through the inclusion of
ceramics in paving and balustrades,
numbers and letters, as well as the
cryptic juxtaposition of inscriptions,
all made by Jujol and incorporated
in some of the ceramics in the form
of a border, offer a clear sample of
Jujol's way of working in respect to
the finish of architectural objects.

Animal symbolisms, disassociated
words with religious connotations, a
surprising play of decontextualization,
are the techniques with which the
young architect throws himself into
the solving of an element as urbane
and utilitarian as an outdoor bench.

One of the most controversial collaborations between Jujol and Gaudí
was their intervention in the work of
moving the choir stalls of the
Cathedral of Mallorca. In accordance
with liturgical tendencies of the mo-

Jujol's intervention in Casa Milà is
also evident. We know of his participation in the finishing work and
more especially in the design of the
ironwork of the balconies, railings
and door in Carrer Provença. In the
locksmith Badia's workshop Jujol
designed with iron cuttings or wires
the shapes that would form each one
of the spectacular joinings that later
made up the large iron railings set on
the façade of the undulating stone.

Jujol here shows his solutions to the
problems of space and continuity
posed by any scale or material. There
is no biographer of Gaudí and Jujol
that does not mention the enthusiasm
with which Gaudí approved the ideas
of his assistant and the delight with
which he, on more than one occasion,
watched Jujol working with iron
strips, sheet iron and wire netting and
saw how the serpentine surfaces which
formed the railings, which would be

ment, the positioning of the choir in the middle of the central aisle was considered inappropriate. Archbishop Campins commissioned Gaudí to move the choir to the Presbytery. In this work Gaudí was accompanied by two of his closest collaborators: Joan Rubió i Bellver, who would be responsible for the statistical studies of the building and who, after disagreements between the Cathedral Chapter and Gaudí, would be responsible for some of the finishing work, and Josep M.ª Jujol to whom Gaudí would entrust the decoration of the *boiserie* of the choir stalls, as well as the solution to the problem of the hanging baldachin over the altar, of the footstool and of some windows in the east façade. The work of the pictorial decoration was so free and creative that, much as it delighted Gaudí who, it seems, urged Jujol to continue, it thoroughly irritated the Cathedral Chapter who were unable to see in those "blotches" anything more than total ugliness and lack of respect. Possibly this produced the breaking point in the already strained relations between the architect (Gaudí) and the client (the Cathedral Chapter) and because of this the decoration of the choir stalls and also the interior of the Cathedral would remain unfinished. Jujol's collaboration with Gaudí was in this case one of the principal reasons why the operation of renovation, whose architectonic interest would have surpassed by far the initial liturgical reason for having commissioned the work, was never completed.

Gaudí and Jujol collaborated on other projects such as The Sagrada Família, the street lights for the Plaça Major (main square) of Vic etc., and it would be appropriate to take advantage of this summary of the relation between them to mention the decisive inverse relation, that is, the influence and teaching of Antoni Gaudí on his young disciple. On examining the work Jujol executed throughout his life, time and time again we find examples of solutions and attitudes that only the overwhelming personality of Gaudí could have produced.

From the most general problems of the handling of materials, the way of thinking about how to build, the deforming and rarefying of typology, to the multitude of details of ironwork, ceramics, woodwork and furniture, all are reminiscent of Gaudí's genius and the impact that, already at the beginning of the century, his method and style had made. This is the legacy that Jujol was to cherish throughout his life and from which he would never attempt to distance himself. But perhaps what is most important at this moment is the fact that the figure Jujol should not, indeed must not, be reduced to that of a mere epigone of Gaudí, for this would give due credit to neither architect. On the contrary, what seems to be most interesting here is evidence of how a way of teaching was from the very start respectful towards the abilities possessed by the disciple, and would throughout the years be assimilated and internalized, producing work as tied to Gaudí as it was autonomous in respect to his teachings.

It was through the radicalization of certain themes and due to his especially characteristic adaptation of the Gaudinian architectural "legacy" that Jujol managed to develop his own working style which shared with that of Gaudí recognition of the crisis in classical architectural culture and of the difficulty in engendering a modern language. In addition to this, however, for Jujol the crisis represented a call to freedom and personal creativity.

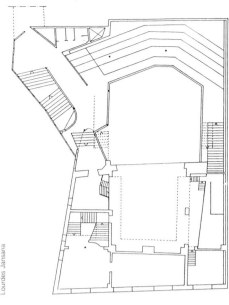

Ground plan of the Teatre del Patronat, Tarragona, 1908 (Drawing by M. Gausa, Archive Quaderns d'Arquitectura).

2.Transformations

Carlos Flores, one of the most intelligent scholars to have studied the collective works of Jujol, has written on several occasions that it is in the transformation of already existing buildings that the creativity and inventiveness of the architect reach their highest peak.

Other scholars of this architect or of his contemporaries have often thought that in the smaller scale works the intervention of the architect was lamentably subject to the limitations of inadequate budgets, that did not allow for the construction of a new ground plan. It is as if new works were, on their own merits, a guarantee of better results, and therefore worthy of more qualified projects.

It is quite the contrary in our case. Due to his special idiosyncrasies and not only to the modest means of his clients, Jujol found special stimulus in situations of intervention in existing structures which enabled him to exercise registers of his sensitivity that were different to those which take precedence in buildings projected and constructed on an empty site.

Does this mean that Jujol had a special talent as a restorer of historical buildings? No such thing can be said, as most of his interventions would certainly not be accepted today by the weighty national trust commissions that watch over the preservation of the architectural heritage of the past.

Firstly, we must recall that a common way of working with already existing buildings from an innovative and creative position was characteristic of architects of that time. Restoration or preservation have little relation to the real transformations carried out by Domènech i Montaner in Canet or in Olot; Puig i Cadafalch in Argentona or in the Plaça de Catalunya in Barcelona; Moncunill in Terrassa; or our architect Jujol in a considerable number of his most representative works.

Secondly, in the case of Jujol, the relation between the existing structure and the intervention seems to have a characteristic value. As we shall see, Jujol always maintains a point of contact between his project and some details of the conditions of the actual work site. These being of historical interest or of existing materials, details which are not only passive references, a contextual framework in which the new work is set, but are true dialectic references, conditions of confrontation in which new constructive organisms are developed.

We can add still another specific characteristic to the numerous transformation jobs carried out by Jujol: the deliberate fragmenting of his specific points of intervention in the body of the previously existing structure.

At other times, in the case of other architects, a more important intervention in an existing building tended to metamorphose all that was previously done, incorporating it into the new order established through a unitary and homogenous language. We can find no instance of this in Jujol's transformation work in which the different incidences act as independent energy nuclei, each having its own logic, developing possibilities established for that problem, in that meeting point of the whole. This is surely one of the most modern aspects of Jujol's work, that which most easily synthesizes with the style and preoccupations of contemporary art and architecture: the acceptance of architectonic action on already existing architectural structures; its incorporation into these being superimposed and localized unbalancing that restructures the strengthening systems — of geometry, of space and color — creating an open structure from the old and the new.

The first transformation work undertaken by Jujol was the conditioning of commercial premises in Carrer Ferran, a central street in Barcelona, where the industrialist and proprietor Pere Manyac had his safe deposit box business (1911).

The starting point of this intervention is the conventional rectangular opening up of the front façade containing the main street entrance and display windows, and the also rectangular area on the ground floor where safes of varying sizes were displayed.

Jujol must have enjoyed the confidence of the proprietor who, being a friend of Gaudí, would not be outraged by the audacious treatment proposed by the architect. The best proof of the goodwill that Manyac felt towards Jujol is to be found in the fact that as from this moment the businessman would become one of Jujol's most assiduous clients.

The operation carried out by Jujol consisted in the manipulation of the woodwork at the entrance, imposing on the conventional division a geometry of diagonal and hexagonal shapes with sloping planes, through the use of which a tense and dynamic structural system was achieved.

This operation of enclosing the entrance was accompanied by a system of flaccid forms, which Carlos Flores has called abstract neo-baroque rehearsed in the decoration of the ceiling of Casa Milà and Casa Batlló, by Gaudí, which in this case is converted into an oozing paste that envelops the ceiling and walls of the interior of the premises.

The shop signs which appear over the main entrance are in relief and in the form of heraldic coats of arms. In these commercial information is combined with the characteristic inclusion of dedications to the Virgin Mary, which are conveyed by casual lettering in the most unlikely places.

The Jujol family archives have preserved a beautiful drawing that sums up the addictive dynamism with which the façade and door to the main entrance were conceived by their author. On a simple sketch of the façade are superimposed schemes, details, decorative solutions of elements, color tests, all of this in a hurried but sure proceeding through which the work is shown as an accumulation of contributions on an existing base which serves as an initial point of departure for the whole project.

Two of the most important works that Jujol carried out in his long career as an architect were those initiated shortly afterwards as transformations of existing buildings. We refer to his prolonged intervention in the Mas Bofarull, in the small town of Els Pallaresos, near Tarragona (1914-1931) and the contemporary work in the Masia Negre in Sant Joan Despí near Barcelona (1915-1927), both rural buildings tied to farming.

The problems involved in both buildings were similar, although the concrete formal solutions adopted were, as we shall see, completely different.

In both cases the construction is similar, being a base of thick masonry walls that subdivides the layout of the ground plan, lacking in regularity or a well-defined symmetrical axis.

In both cases, on the part of the client there was a desire to renovate the building along the lines of Palladian villas, making of a farmhouse not only a place for active production but also an environment symbolizing the social status and economic power of the country landowner.

The work of the architect in both Els Pallaresos and Sant Joan Despí was to be in the nature of an "adjustment" *(arreglo)*, an expression that characterizes a certain way of understanding the role of the architect, not so much as an inventor of a new structure, but as someone capable of enhancing the most representative values of a structure or building that already exists.

In both cases the alteration works lasted a long time, decades in fact, so that the design process was highly susceptible to variations, changes and corrections. In this way the underlying temporariness of the work is patently clear in the way the whole alteration process developed.

In Els Pallaresos Jujol received the commission from the owners, the sisters Pepita and Dolores Bofarull, long-standing acquaintances whom Jujol had met in the village of La Secuita, where for several years previously he had spent his summer holidays.

Josep M.ª Jujol, son and biographer of our architect, points out that the idea behind the commission his father received was to "eliminate the neglected appearance of the house and ennoble it."

Jujol's intervention in the Mas Bofarull is not easy to summarize due to the multiplicity of his contributions on so many different levels. However, as far as the renewed physiognomy of the house was concerned, some fundamental decisions were taken at project level that affected the overall shape of the building. The most important of these was the renovation of the staircase, center of vertical communication in the house, placed on the site of an already existing stairway; this would be converted into a central space in the whole interior system of the building. The staircase is set in a square body, which as it rises forms an open vertical shape which is projected above the roof of the old country house and ascends in the form of a graceful openwork tower, topped by a four-sided sloping roof over which seems to hover the imposing but light figure of an angel, designed by Jujol himself.

As it rises, the tower changes in shape from being square to hexagonal, producing with this geometric figure a small opening through which a beam of light descends, acquiring iridescence thanks to the diversity of color tones in which the ceiling, walls, banisters and railings are painted.

In the part that emerges above the main roof of the house, the tower breaks away from its parallepipedic shapes with windows set at angles and with some openings at its highest point that respond to the concentration of the support system, precisely at the previously mentioned angles, of the ceramic covered cowl roof.

Also the most westerly angle of the building is embellished in the form of a turret topped by some fantastically simplified battlements, with a free and varied treatment of crenellations in which neither the enchanting balconies with their railings made of twisted metal rods nor the corner windows which are fitted into the arris of the tower are missing.

Delimited by this large fortified tower and in the front of the back façade, on the west side of the building, Jujol constructed a third element which is of especial significance

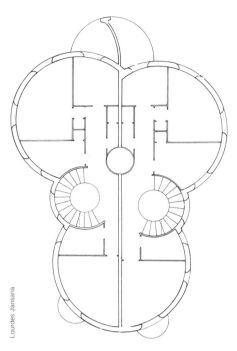

First floor of the Torre de la Creu, Sant Joan Despí (Barcelona), 1913 (Drawing M. Gausa. Archive Quaderns d'Arquitectura).

Lourdes Jansana

La Torre de la Creu in construction, Sant Joan Despí (Barcelona), around 1913 (Jujol Archive).

in this renovation: the light brick-work gallery supported on fragile cast iron columns. It is the most historical piece of the whole work: a reappraisal of the theme of classical galleries added to country houses in the XVII and XVIII centuries, here treated in a hybrid manner which is somewhere between Gothic and the Nazarene. All the creative potential inherent in the knowledge Jujol acquired of the construction possibilities of brick is lavished on this brocade of ceramic, the red façade of the gallery, which stands in marked contrast to the white stucco of the towers.

Another point of interest in the house is the garden at the rear, with its imaginative treatment of divisions and enclosing wall. No less interesting is the intervention in the annex which is destined as a wash house, where Jujol introduced parabolic arches which form a pergola, at the same time providing the solution to the problem of the new doors for carriages and pedestrians through a daringly asymmetrical use of forms and material.

If from the architectural interventions we pass to the decorative details, Mas Bofarull is perhaps the work that is richest in glasswork, railings, doors, windows, furniture, floors and all kinds of imaginative contributions made at different times and also a result of different suggestions.

Thanks as much to the loving care with which this building has been maintained up to the present day by the owners, as to Jujol's lavish outlay of genius for a period of almost twenty years, there is no doubt that this is one of the architect's most representative and complete works.

In the Masia Negre, the placing of a new staircase was a key operation in the remodeling of the interior of the building. Both this and the new silhouette of the façade were the first steps towards the ennobling of a discreet *masia* (country mansion) situated on what were then the outskirts of the small agricultural town of Sant Joan Despí. Jujol began working on the Torre de la Creu in 1913, in the same town in which he would finally become Municipal architect, and where he constructed a number of buildings. The lawyer Pere Negre i Jover had his practice in Barcelona but kept up production on his large estates in the town where he was born. It was through his family relations that he came into contact with Jujol, whom he commissioned to renovate his house. Almost all of what is fundamental to this project is to be found on a blue envelope that later Jujol would cut up, following the outline of the façade, using his prodigious skill for representation through the shapes of cut-out paper.

On the façade Jujol proposed the introduction of a new profile of the steeple, evoking the serpentine shape of the baroque façades of many Catalan *masias* renovated at the time. The sinuous quality of the symmetrical baroque curves would be changed here into an undulating outline, irregular, delicately sloping, like a graceful gesture of the hand, designed to disguise the untidy sequence of hollows on the existing façade. In the project, this characteristic outline is completed with sinuous calligraphy on the façade, running over the impost which was set at the level of the first floor and incorporating garlands and medallions with written allusions (in Latin) to the text of the Ave Maria.

Two artifacts are superimposed on the free background of stucco and sgraffiti, these being a glassed-in observatory and its balconies on either side placed over the front door; its design was inspired by the traditional "tartana," the typical country horse-drawn carriage, to which Jujol gave a significance which was not only the obvious meaning in the rural context of the building, but also the symbolism of the vehicle that, modestly but reliably, would carry the inhabitants of the house to heavenly glory through meditation on the Virgin Mary.

Another significant element, although this was never built, was the exterior flight of stairs that would join the first floor directly to the old esplanade at the front of the house. Bow windows, oval windows, stone benches on either side of the front door, were among the other elements

incorporated into an elegant and at the same time hieroglyphic façade.

Inside the house, Jujol's intervention is specific and limited, thus creating an effect of centers of architectural operations, with the belief that thanks to these strong points of intensive architectural activity the overall transformation of the building would be achieved, without the necessity of carrying out a complete treatment of renovation on the building.

Outstanding amongst these nuclei of intervention are the ensemble of the main staircase, covered by a spiral octagonal-shaped dome, and the elliptical chapel situated on the first floor, which is topped by an also elliptical skylight, whose openings admit the sunlight at a slanting angle.

The solution of both pieces is as sumptuous as it is economical. There is neither a lavish use of materials nor daring structures. It is the ingenious combination of a wooden structure for the stairway with the skilful project for the eight-sided skylight, made with simple wooden beams and ceramic vaults and finished in luxurious blue and white stucco that gives a fascinating aspect to the space that ascends to the first floor.

In the chapel, on the other hand, it is the delicate treatment of the velvet which covers the walls that ushers us into a kaleidoscope of golds, blues and whites. The reminiscence of baroque cupolas is only a remote reference to a personal interpretation in which the "horror vacui" runs parallel to the unquenchable inventive capacity of the architect, even in the tiniest details.

In the back garden, in the side windows, in the metal iron gate set in one of the sides of the main façade, in the parabolic arches that form a pergola in front of the building, Jujol has left a wealth of samples of a misplaced genius, confirming once again that his prodigious gifts as a designer of details found their element when presented with the challenge of working on an already-existing architectural structure.

There is another of Jujol's renovation works, today in an unhappily precarious state of preservation, that must be considered as important. This

is the addition of a chamber dedicated to the Virgen del Carmen in the chapel of the Convent de les Carmelites in the city of Tarragona.

In 1917 a contest was held for the completion of the chamber, which had already been started. It was probably because of his connection with the city in which he had been born and also with the promoters of the contest, that Jujol prepared the project that would be chosen by the Jury in 1918.

The project consisted of the addition to the octagonal body set in the prolongation of the main axis of the neo-Gothic church of the Carmelite Fathers. A wide space topped by a dome admitted a statue of the Virgin Mary set in an elevated position, access to which would be by way of a symmetrical double flight of steps situated on both sides of the main axis. On top of the dome a slender steeple formed a second space, also octagonal, made up of a system of radial buttresses whose piers were to be filled in with stained glass.

It was, in this case, a more canonic intervention than those previously carried out by Jujol. It was based on an established model: votive Gothic chapels such as had flourished around the ambulatories of medieval cathedrals. Here it would be appropriate to emphasize how similar Jujol's approach was to that of types of transformations characteristic of other ages, and how it revealed his own points of interest. On the other hand, in the redesign of the adapted historical model, the modifications introduced regarding the vertical illumination through the construction of the skylight or in the sumptuous decoration is more reminiscent of the transparent baroque than the structural mouldings of the neo-Gothic of Viollet-le-Duc.

Diametrically opposed to this intervention is that which, at the same time, Jujol was engaged on in another house in the aforementioned town of Els Pallaresos. We refer to the work done for the widow Fortuny in her house which was in front of the village church, and was commonly known as Ca l'Andreu.

Interiors for the first floor of the Casa
Batlló, Barcelona, 1906 (Jujol Archive).

This is yet another example of a project in which a series of different architectural interventions was required: the remodeling of the façade (only partially carried out), the redesigning of the vestibule for carriages and the base of the stairway leading to the first floor; the design of the central piece destined for the dining-room; furniture, flooring, woodwork, and objects of household use.

It is worth pointing out the materials employed in this intervention and the way in which they were used to achieve luxurious and brilliant effects, based on solutions full of simplicity and skill: the front door covered in sheet copper and studded with a design that is reminiscent of the cross of Saint Andrew, the flooring of the entrance hall, or the treatment of the woodwork of the large windows, all occupy a prominent position in the gallery of Jujol's master works.

We could also mention the many other works in which in the hands of Jujol this unique transforming process produced results that are enormously efficient, particularly those of some chapels and hermitages like those of Lloret (1926) in the municipality of Renau or in the Hermitage of Roser (1927) in Vallmoll, where some delicate and modest modifications to the façade and in the interior have produced results of exquisite quality

and where, once again, the intuitive sensitivity of our architect is demonstrated on detecting the points where an intense application of design would produce effects that are greater than the actual elements which are being modified.

Also in the very long list of interventions carried out after the Civil War, in churches that had been devastated during the Revolution and the war, Jujol's work bears the same signature: among others the parish church of Sant Joan Despí (1943-1949); that of Sant Salvador in Vendrell (1939-1949); and of Guimerà (1940-1945); Bonastre (1941-1945) or that of Els Pallaresos (1941-1944) which culminates his work in the town. The specific localized action of Jujol's design confirms a method of working whereby the particular seems to be the instrument through which the global effects of architectural transformation are achieved.

3.Houses

In Jujol we encounter two housing traditions: on the one hand, the one represented by Gaudí, who undoubtedly had an influence on our architect, according to which the construction of the building is above all a controversial and critical operation. On the other hand, several of Jujol's houses seem to have an air of *noucentisme* about them, thus conferring greater importance on the dwelling and where the approach to the anonymous and popular represents one of the ideological starting points through which the idea of the house is developed.

Gaudí's experience in housing construction is of considerable importance, despite the fact that houses occupied a position of lesser significance in the system of values of our maestro from Reus. The fact is that throughout his life Gaudí constructed a great number of houses. He did so with great determination and in such a way that these experiences allowed him to lay down strategies with which he could deal with the residential problem.

Blocks of flats are a phenomenon that seems to contradict the notion of habitable space according to classical and academic traditions. The block of flats in the *Eixample* (19th-century extension) of Barcelona or in any other place, has to be a unique building, in spite of its collective character. The monumentalization of the residential building is a way of reacting critically against urban monotony and anonymity. On the other hand, according to the Gaudí tradition, the typology of a tenement house has to be manipulated, its standardization distorted so as to emphasize the exceptional elements which are not repeated on a global scale. Doorways, flights of steps, turrets or symmetrical centers and indoor courtyards all are suitable elements by means of which to enhance the unitary value of the building.

Finally, the house as a home, collective or individual, is a pious place in which faith should be embodied in

Façade for Manyac shop, Barcelona, 1911 (Jujol Archive).

Lourdes Jansana

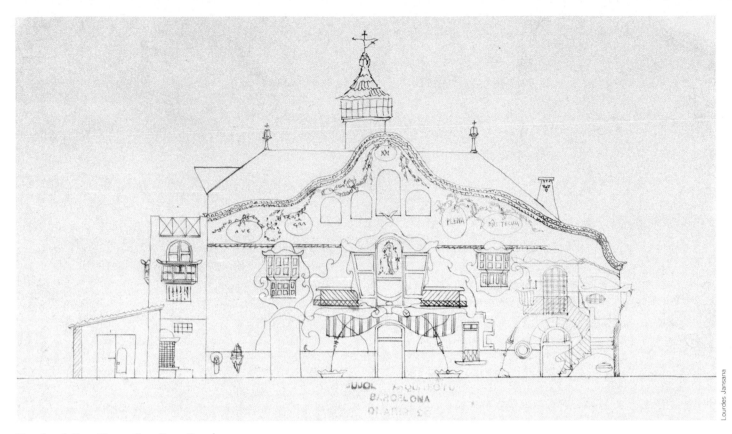

Façade of Casa Negre, Sant Joan Despí
(Barcelona), 1915 (Jujol Archive).

construction as a manifestation of praise. While a house is not a temple, it should nevertheless be a major element in the tireless uplifting of a Christian city.

All these characteristics are to be found in the few but important tenement buildings planned by Jujol. His conception of a collective house, his participation in Gaudí's Batlló and Milà houses, and his own building projects clearly reveal that he was a faithful follower of critical reform and express a deep dissatisfaction with the characteristics of the modern city.

But there is in Jujol another component which has nothing whatsoever to do with Gaudí and which only appears in his work with personal modulations as his career advances. The house of *Noucentisme*, the movement to which Jujol was a contemporary, represents an essential part of political and cultural projects of that time. Due to the influence of Anglo-Saxon policy regarding housing, the perfect *noucentista* house is the individual detached house situated in a discreet garden, far away from urban density and exalting suburban equilibrium.

Gaudí and his circle were by no means foreign to Ruskin or to the diffusion of his ideas by the members of the "Societat Cívica de la Ciutat Jardí." The ideal artisan house is one of well programmed construction, minimized, without drawing from problems concerning style, and comfortably characterized by the confluence of true Mediterraneanism and the retrieval of the anonymous house by master builders. Jujol shared these ideals, as can be seen above all in the sumptuous houses he built in the suburbs of Sant Joan Despí, Cornellà and Barcelona.

A publication by Montserrat Duran i Albareda painstakingly documents the architectural work carried out by Jujol in the municipality of Sant Joan Despí and its surroundings, precisely in the years when this farming town became part of the outskirts of the city, offering residence, town or country houses to the citizens of the metropolis. Jujol became the municipal architect of this small town in 1926, but his work extends from the assignment of the "Torre de la Creu," in 1913, till the today non-existent offices for the Caixa de Pensions which were left incomplete in 1949, the year of his death. More than fifty projects, amongst which we find both alterations and new buildings, were concerned with the subject of housing. In many cases architectural interest in these buildings is limited to details, small expressions, delicate modifications of the stereotypes established by the master builders. But the conclusion one reaches when looking over this extensive work of lesser importance is not that Jujol led a professional double life, with "architectural" projects in some cases, and in others simple legitimizations of unscrupulous practices, but that there is a continuity in all his works. Thus, his most humble buildings provide us with keys to an understanding of his more committed ones and enable us to see the survival of an ideal of discretion, a simple life, a love of details, a preference for the small scale, control of ornamentation, coloring, presence of nature, all these things being part of a lifestyle, which, if not strictly that of *Noucentisme*, in the literal, classical sense, certainly represents the peaceful ideal of the house as an individualized entity on the outskirts of the big city.

Among the collective houses planned by Jujol, special mention should be made of Casa Ximenis in Tarragona (1914), the project for Joan Boix in Barcelona (1919), which was never carried out, and above all Casa Planelles, also in Barcelona, the subject of several projects and finally begun in 1923.

While the first two are transformations of already existing buildings, it would nevertheless be more exact to consider them alongside completely new constructions, as the previously existing building in both cases had only a minor role to play in the new project.

The interest of Casa Ximenis lies fundamentally in the calligraphy on the façade overlooking the Rambla, as here one can discern, if only in a superficial way, the Gaudinian tendency to distort the established characteristics of the façade through the brilliantly skilful design of sgraffiti, windows and balconies.

In the housing project for Joan Boix, the external operation is also centred on large windows and balconies, paying very special attention to the positioning of a religious figure at the highest point of the corner, thus defining the pious will manifest in any of Jujol's works, not only in those fulfilling an explicitly liturgical purpose.

However, the most ambitious of all the blocks of flats built by Jujol is undoubtedly the one situated on a triangular piece of ground delimited by Avinguda Diagonal and Carrer de Sicília, executed for the building contractor and promoter Evelí Planelles.

Josep M.ª Jujol jr., son and biographer of our architect, explains how the three consecutive projects for this site developed between 1922 and 1923. One should not be surprised to see that the first proposal was for a single-family house with a garden. Although the site was so central, Jujol's discomfort when faced with the subject of collective housing led him to choose types found in garden cities. The second proposal was also a one-family house, but with greater exploitation of the building ground on this corner, whose importance was exceptional, due to the intersection of three large streets according to the plan for Barcelona by Cerdà. The architectural proposal was "an authentic sculpture fit to live in." Jujol's deep religious beliefs led him to propose an enormous figure of the Immaculate Conception, standing on a great pedestal which was in fact the house itself. Allegories on the name of Jesus and all kinds of symbolic elements would make the house disappear behind the religious figure of the monument. Due probably to pressure on the part of Planelles, who while a friend and sympathizer of Jujol's was also his client and himself a builder, the third project was a reminiscence, on a smaller scale, of the original idea for Casa Milà: a continuous and undulating structure whose ascending growth reached its peak at the corner of the two streets. The solution was expressed through a clear distinction between the base formed by the ground floor and the entresol, the first

floor with an important part of its surface opening up on the sides, thanks to a spectacular belvedere with bay windows, and the upper floors, all the same, crowned by a top part of more reduced dimensions.

The decorative details of the building were only partially Jujol's responsibility, which means that the splendour of the details of the banisters, the gratings and the stucco on the ceilings disappears on the top floors. On contemplating this building, and taking into account the time when it was constructed, it is hard to avoid drawing a parallel with the Expressionism of the German architect Mendelsohn. Knowing Jujol's evolution and also the vicissitudes in the development of the ornamentation which had been designated for this building, it seems daring to want to find an easy connection between the architect from Berlin and the Catalan. There certainly was an explicit affinity between Gaudí and the Expressionists which cannot be ignored, although we can be almost certain that Jujol knew nothing about his German colleague. The only fair conclusion considering this suggestion of similarity would be to say that their respective undertakings had much in common. Both Gaudí and his circle and the Expressionists were critical of the modern city and of classical tradition. Their conception of shape was abstract and they were inspired by nature. Perhaps it would be these common attitudes that best might help to explain an analogy which, on the other hand, cannot be put down to any direct influence.

Jujol's experience regarding the detached house is much more extensive and indicates his withdrawal from Gaudí's influence and his personal work with the ideals of *Noucentisme* by an architect, whom we can link only very obliquely to this cultural project.

The first house built by Jujol, and one of the first buildings projected by him after the years of direct collaboration with Gaudí, is the Torre San Salvador which he built in 1909 for his friend Doctor Salvador San

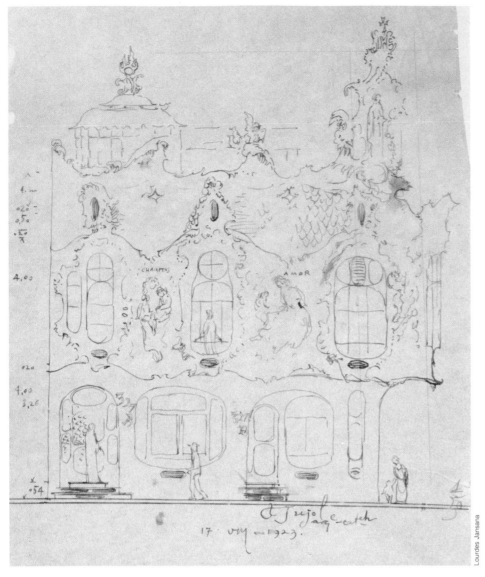

Façade of Casa Planelles, Barcelona, 1923
(Jujol Archive).

of the water, which made him decide to market it under the name of "Agua Radial." This change of course thwarted the project of the building, which was subsequently adapted to its new industrial use.

Years later, in 1917, Jujol received the commission to build in another part of the same estate a second single-family house, which was to be called Torre Queralt. Here too, it is a case of a regular ground plan with two levels, on which, in a very striking way the entrance door and a balcony disrupt the arris of one of the angles of the building, thus producing an effect of brutal contrast between geometry of different scale and aspect similar to what was achieved with Els Pallaresos at about the same time.

The finish of the railings and the crests is more delicate and less crude, in such a way that the overall impression of the house, including the enclosing wall, is more harmonious than that of the first house, even though geometrical contrasts begin to manifest themselves as one of the most characteristic resources of our architect when building family houses.

The peculiar Torre de la Creu, commonly known as the Casa dels Ous (House of Eggs), due precisely to the total prevalence of curvilinear forms in its composition, could be labelled as a geometrical manifesto. It was commissioned by Doña Josefa Romeu, the architect's aunt, who in this way provided her nephew with the opportunity of complete freedom when planning a holiday home to be built in Sant Joan Despí, a municipality where Jujol would later execute a great amount of his work. The project was begun in 1913 and construction lasted till the summer of 1916. The house, divided vertically into two separate dwellings with one main entrance and a garden, was situated on a piece of land of limited dimensions (527 m²), typical of the type of residential ground distribution to which we have already referred. The interesting aspects of the house lie in the experimental idea of shape and construction based on the assembly of five cylindrical prisms placed along a longitudinal wall serving as an axis,

Salvador on a site situated on the hill of Ntra. Sra. del Coll in Barcelona.

When Jujol built this house he was still involved with the works in the Park Güell, and we must not forget that even the geographical proximity of the two sites established a relationship which is also formally recognizable. The doctor's house was a simple building where the most important ornamental features were the sgraffiti, the flooring and the windows as well as the sloping hilly garden, the surrounding wall and the metal gate. Jujol transformed an initially simple plan and shape into a recital of *divertimenti* with each architectural incident he had to face. The house was not entirely finished, as during the sinking of a well which was to provide the property with water, the owner discovered the curative effects although the layout of the different circular shapes involves a slight displacement which cuts through the rigidity of what otherwise might have been perfect symmetry. Of the five cylinders, three are of greater diameter and correspond to the different rooms on the three superimposed levels. The two smaller cylinders correspond to the spiral wells for the two staircases, each of which serves one of the two dwellings which make up the whole house.

On the ground floor the drawing-room of the two flats is situated in the cylinder which is positioned on the main dividing axis of the building.

The interior circular space grows dynamically towards the exterior, through a glazed perimetric gallery which widens the cylindrical shape at the base.

At the top of the main cylinders a cornice with an imprecise outline and gentle curvatures crowns the aforementioned shapes, which at the top have a delicate cobweb of thin metal bars forming a kind of balustrade, and a system of egg-shaped cupolas which cover the central part of each of the bodies.

The staircase cylinders are of different heights, also a motive for unexpected variety, and are covered by wide cowls of a tiled vault structure, with jutting eaves in the same material, supported by free-standing, stuccoed brick masonry uprights.

From the constructional point of view, the building is proof of the versatility and possibilities of ceramic brick, since this is the material used for the walls, the arches, the door posts, the segmental arches in the doors and windows, the circles and the crests, as well as for the floor-tiles, the narrow ceiling vaults between beams, and the two spiral stairwells.

But it is also in this building that Jujol began the large-scale use of two techniques which were to become fundamental to him when structuring the image of the house. First of all stucco, normally white, pressed when hot, using a traditional, economic, and efficient solution in harmony with the *noucentista* taste for smooth and taut surfaces, as produced by a great

Lourdes Jansana

Interior view of the Cambril del Carme, Tarragona, 1919 (Jujol Archive).

Interior of the Casa Andreu, Els Pallaresos (Tarragona), 1923 (Jujol Archive).

number of contemporary architects. He would then apply sgraffiti to the stucco, which enabled Jujol to give free rein to his taste for calligraphy, sign painting, iconographic decoration and the evocation of pious themes.

Secondly, there are the lush colors of ceramics and mosaic. The domes of Torre de la Creu can be seen from a considerable distance, thanks to the intense color that covers them. Jujol achieved this through the use of glass residue which had been obtained from a nearby glassworks. Problems of adhesion and lack of maintenance caused the destruction of a good deal of this characteristic coating which was substituted by ceramics made and put in place by one of the architect's daughters more than twenty years ago.

But it is doubtlessly in the ironwork of the railings and grids where the brilliance of the architect comes closest to present-day tastes.

Iron hoops, sheets, rings knotted like string, diagonal paths, and meandering forms produced by an expression of free movement are amongst the most exciting aspects of Jujol's outstanding work in this field.

Straddling constructive experiments and the introduction of homeliness as a scale and value, the Casa dels Ous should be considered as the veritable turning point between Gaudí's legacy and Jujol's highly personal way of tackling the construction of a house.

Having seen this building, it is easier to comprehend the small houses that can still be seen in the same town. Some of them are in a deplorable condition. Others have been demolished. Very few of them are recognizable. Not one of them has been restored with dignity.

During the twenties Jujol constructed a considerable number of one-family houses on the outskirts. Some of them detached, surrounded by a small garden. Others semi-detached with one or two floors where Jujol's contribution is only discernible through some decorative feature, a delicate superposition or a disturbing displacement.

As Manuel Gausa has pointed out in an interesting survey of some of Ju-

jol's houses, the Casa Serra-Xaus, built in 1921, sets out from a rectangular system made up by a displaced double-square, in whose diagonals 45° turns are produced with respect to other, smaller regular elements.

What causes surprise in this house is the contrast between the daring geometry and the homeliness of the size and surface treatment. Renouncing more committed operations, the plan stakes everything on the emphasis put on the access to the house from the chamfered corner. A powerful rostrum turned 45° on the diagonal axis is placed like a displaced cube, but in the same position as the whole volume of the building. The effect, despite the planned turret not having been built, which would have reinforced the point of rotation and the displacement produced on the corner, is of a striking geometry, which once again takes us back to Jujol's formal experiments which we have already seen in previous works.

How can this set of disrupted and displaced shapes coexist with the white stucco, the gentle floral sgraffiti and the bright blue of the woodwork?

All the iconography of *Noucentisme* seems to settle in a geometry that in no way is the delicate composition between classicism and the vernacular, favored by the architects of small contemporary houses built on the periphery.

Opposite Casa Serra-Xaus, on the other side of the street, Jujol built a two-family house for his family and other possible tenants. The site is rectangular, its longer side running parallel to one of the streets. The arrangement of the two-family house is the result of arranging a ground plan in the shape of a "T," in contiguity with two dwellings forming an "L." Jujol's ground plan here is one of his finest architectural achievements. Displaying a symmetry which is rigid in the central core and diversified in the side wings, a dominating horizontal movement against which the vertical emergence of the central part is set, a free-and-easy way of arranging the tilted roof of the different parts of the building, resolving the pro-

View of the Casa Bofarull,
Els Pallaresos (Tarragona), 1914
(Jujol Archive).

blems of the independence of the two flats, using refined and highly economical solutions for the facing, the stucco of the windows, woodwork and flooring, Jujol here achieves, in our opinion, one of his masterpieces.

Probably Jujol's urge to experiment had died down somewhat by the thirties. While the conquest of domesticity had not made him renounce his ability to manipulate form, this skill now became exquisitely constructive, carefully logical, dimensionally welcoming; no longer was there a need to use the house as a laboratory for geometrical experiments, rotations and displacements, to which the architect probably no longer conceded a pre-eminent role.

The carrying out of numerous realistic and modest assignments of so many houses in the twenties in the streets of Montjuïc (1926), Jacint Verdaguer (1926), Frederic Casas (1930), Francesc Macià (1931) or in the isolated buildings such as Torre Camprubí (1928), Dot Carrera (1929), Mas Roseta (1930), Zaragoza (1931) or Passahi (1931) had changed the balance between the problem of shape and the idea of the home. It was, in a sense, the testament of an outsider in architecture facing the uncompromising architectural problem of the house.

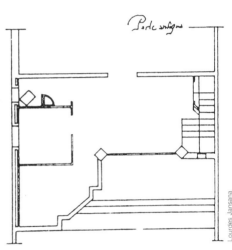

Extension of La Casa Dot, Sant Joan Despí (Barcelona), 1926 (Drawing by M. Gausa. Quaderns d'Arquitectura Archive).

Lourdes Jansana

4.Structures

Gaudí's followers had learnt from their maestro how essential the structural conception is to architecture. This reasoning, which had been inherited from 19th-century technological Rationalism, had become the centre of formal contemplation when it came to facing monumental problems. The ennoblement of a country house is also an architectural problem. For Jujol and Gaudí's followers the classical idea of decorum still persisted as something more than an added value. According to the classical Albertian tradition, it is architecture's contribution to the dignity of social life. But in large public edifices architecture should show its splendour not only through the grace of its decorative discoveries, but also, and above all, through the congruence of forms based on a solid structural and constructional logic.

The conceptual tradition according to which Jujol had been trained sprang from the debate about the future of architecture begun by Eugène Viollet-le-Duc. Those who think the French essayist was merely a historian of medieval architecture, inciting all kinds of Gothic revivals, are mistaken. On the pages of the *Dictionnaire* or the *Entretiens* the key question, subject to debate and reflection, is the architecture of the future. It can be reached only by overcoming stylistic repertoires and going into a deeper study of rational perfection of building and the structural organisms on which the enclosure of a space is sustained.

In Gaudí's circle the problem of the structural organism was at the very centre of the architectural debate, the *sine qua non* condition of a monumental architecture worthy of such a name. It is therefore not surprising that also in Jujol's case the problem of structure is more of a main issue for public buildings than for private ones. Surely there are always signs of structural and constructive talent in most of his works, but in this kind of building, in a house, the fundamental is the precinct and the

physiognomy, the countenance and the appearance of the building. On the other hand in a public building, the structure, its logic and coherence are not a matter decided by image but the other way round, the result of an internal consideration.

This priority given to the structural-constructive takes on an even more decisive importance in the building of churches. The temple, as this kind of building is very often called by Gaudí's followers, is the crucial matter of architecture. It is and has been the origin and the résumé of all the problems related to this discipline throughout history. The perfection of each type of architecture throughout history has been materialized in an exemplary way in its concept of the temple and of the structural logic established to build it. In a way, the architecture of the two completely new churches projected by Jujol, and despite (or perhaps thanks to) the economic limits that were imposed on them, constitutes the extension of a by no means modern aesthetic idea, with theological roots, if when using this terminology we mean all that in thoughts and in practice originates not from a theocentrical conception of the world but from lay humanism.

Jujol received his first commission to build a completely new building when he was still working full-time with Gaudí. This was the theater for the Patronat de l'Obrer (Workers' Association), a typical institution founded by clerical groups through which they sought to "raise the cultural, moral and religious level of the workers," part of a paternalistic policy unable to comprehend the social problems of industrial cities.

Jujol's biographers have insisted on the symbolic intention of this building, thus emphasizing the idea that "the stage and the auditorium would be like the ship of the Roman Catholic Church, sailing and fighting against the waves of life."

Certainly there are some allusions to sailing and the sea in the interior decoration, but some experiments with structure facing the problem of a large space intended for performances strike us as being of far greater interest.

From this point of view, there are two contributions which stand out. On the one hand, the organization of the system of interior spaces (the Workers' Association theater is practically no more than an interior) through the complex layout of the flights of steps and the rows of seats in the dress circle. Once again, we must allude to the modesty of the project and the immediacy with which Jujol adopts the characteristics of a theater as his starting point: a parallelepipedic area with a rectangular pit and a high gallery at the end of the auditorium. But this simple formula, which at no point clashes with more high-flying historical models, is enriched by the fluency of the different flights of stairs, the connection with the dress-circle area in an open polygonal shape, and above all by the structural decisions linked to qualitative changes designed to improve conventional typologies. The use of a light structure of columns made of cast iron, slanted metal joists and tiled vaults, slanted as well, is a solution just as daring as it is fraught with problems. In any case we would like to emphasize Jujol's will to change the characteristics through structural experiments in the rows of seats of the dress-circle as well as the flights of steps or the front of the stage, all of which constitute the most innovative elements in the project.

Jujol certainly displays all the possibilities of his prodigious talent in the details and the finish. But the experimenting with a metal structure for an unusual situation, the incorporation of the ornamentation to this basic structure show us a Jujol who is very close to the structural and decorative experiments carried out by Gaudí and Jujol himself at about the same time in Casa Milà in Barcelona.

Even more decisive in the conception of a building is Jujol's choice of structure for the locksmith's shop that he built in 1916 for this client Pere Manyac in Riera de Sant Miquel in the Gràcia district in Barcelona.

Those architects who were children of the tradition of *Modernisme* felt obliged to flirt with metal structures, since this was *de rigueur*, above all if we consider how their possibilities had been raised to almost mythological heights by the aforementioned Viollet-le-Duc. But it is also true that the way of understanding these structures was conceived in analogy to an invented interpretation of Gothic structures. A truss which obtains its stability through the joining of the bars which close in a three-dimensional fashion and a system of skeleton which, the lighter and more versatile, the more efficient it is. The revival of buildings with partition *a la catalana* is considered to be the vestiges of a traditional way of building, but the fact is that tradition has little to do with the way of erecting buildings having a metal structure, as far as the overall performance of the structure is concerned.

Nevertheless, Gaudí's circle maintained a more reserved attitude regarding the monumental use of metal structures, and the fact is that in Gaudí's work this appears only in places which could be defined as secondary, auxiliary, of lesser importance. Great monumental architecture should be based solely on the tradition of compressed structures, of stone, masonry or brick.

Due to its industrial nature, Manyac's factory is perhaps the clearest case of Jujol's confronting a building of metal structure. His answer is exemplary: a framework of steel profiles closed in with glass and partition vaults. It was the stretching of this repertory to its limits that caused one of the vaulted sections to fall down, an event which upset Jujol deeply. His answer to the difficulty was "Gothic": trusses and the use of buttresses converted into magic devices made of brick, which, like earflaps, stuck out on top of the broken profile of the "shed" roof. Inside the building, the wise and surprising use of his usual curved shapes, large oval windows, undulating forms which, in the skylights and above the handbasin changed into fantastic forms and shapes which seemed to float in the open transparency of the bays.

Taking everything into account, among all the monumental works carried out by Josep M.ª Jujol the one par excellence was the Sagrat Cor church in Vistabella. When we say monumental, we use this term in the sense it had in Gaudí's circle, that is: the splendour of a structure consecrated to worshipping, in which the distinction between what supports and what is supported tends to disappear.

Vistabella is a hamlet which belongs to the municipality of La Secuita, in the heart of the *Camp de Tarragona*. The decision to build a small church in the village was based on an initiative by some individuals and the parish priest. It is, as is usual in our architect, the case of a building of reduced size, constructed with limited resources but in which Jujol would display his fullest knowledge in a complete and unitary piece of work.

The project was begun in 1918 and the consecration of the almost finished church took place in 1923. It was built by some stone masons and in collaboration with the village people. The costs were, to a great extent, met by monetary donations, or paid in kind by the parishioners themselves or by farming landowners in the area. The shape of the building is, in its conception, elementary. Large intersecting vaults with parabolic arches which spring from four free-standing pilasters. From this initial core the lateral spaces appear like a cascade, four of them corresponding to the direction of the diagonal axes that cross the keystone of the main vault. On the larger axis, these diagonal spaces make up the presbytery with the altar, and on the opposite side, the entrance door above which the choir gallery is to be found. On the minor axis, both lateral chapels form a virtual transept. The building is located on a square enclosure which is turned at 45° in relation to the axis of the main intersecting vault. This square extends on two of its sides to encompass the baptismal chapel, the sacristy and the residence of the parish priest. On the main axis the structure of the entrance porch is also an intersecting vault with parabolic arches, displaced corresponding to the men-

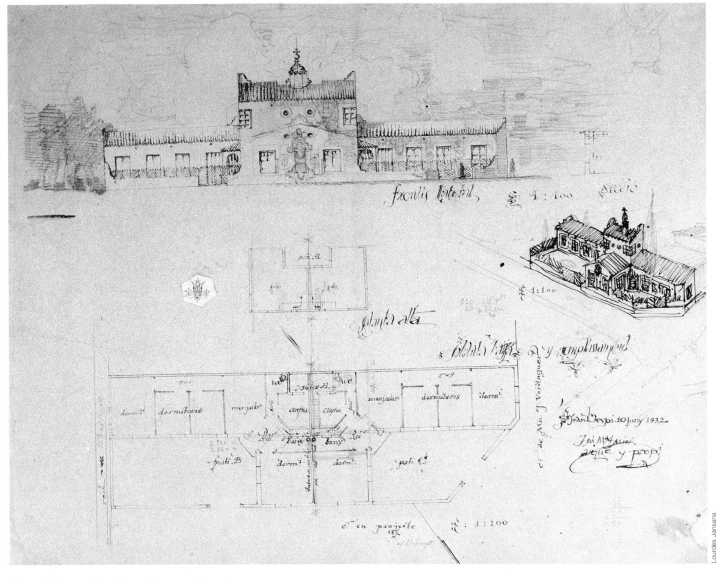

Ground plans, side view and perspective of
La Casa Jujol in Sant Joan Despí
(Barcelona), 1932 (Jujol Archive).

tioned axis, thus producing a diagonal intersection on one of the angles of the surrounding square.

A similar procedure defines the Capella del Santíssim, set at one of the ends of the secondary axis.

From the keystone of the main vault a very high steeple rises, being hexagonal at the base and becoming triangular as it ascends, in such a way that the top three thinning walls meet at the central vertical axis of the building, like buttresses, whose arisses virtually form a kind of pyramid with a triangular base.

The walls that make up the base of the building are of masonry and double tiled vaults in the roofing of the aisles. Jujol proudly insists on this traditional solution of terraced roofs, applied to a vaulted form, as doing this leaves the forms of the vaults bare in the exterior, without any need for a roof, but thanks to the vacuum chamber between both layers of tile sheets solving the problem of humidity, condensation and the stability of the roof caps. The whole of the exterior is finished in its natural texture, without stucco or facing. On the exterior everything is finished in its natural texture, with neither stucco nor facing of any kind, while inside, the parabolic arches are of brick with elements of stone incorporated, and the pilasters that form the base are a mixture of ashlars and brick.

The interior walls are stuccoed to accommodate the luxurious mural decoration projected by Jujol himself and to a great extent carried out by him as well.

Only by carefully analysing the structural composition of the building can we understand the severity of its formal unity, surpassing the first impression of a tangle of overlaying elements, which is what the unanalytical eye sees.

The fact is that Jujol, as his son explains so often in his aforementioned biography, set out from an idea which was as elementary as it was unitary. He says that only a few days after receiving the commission, Jujol showed the promoters of the building of the church a simple model made up of the crossing of metal bars which formed parabolic arches. "The bell tower will be here" said the architect indicating a point in space above the crossing of the two arches, and with this everything was decided.

From a theoretical point of view, the architectural and liturgical debate of the Christian church, in which the Gaudí circle joined enthusiastically, has two aspects. On the one hand, the difficulty of a compromise between the unity of the central ground plan and the diversity of the cruciform plan. Basilica or pantheon, western Christian tradition or oriental. These are the extremes of the problem whose consequences in the sense of interior space are evident. But this argument, typological if you wish, is linked to the problem of structure and construction. For the church, the fragmentary procedure that we have analysed in Jujol's transformation work is not applicable. The demands of radical unity are the primary requirements of monumental structures. In the case of Vistabella, the unity is achieved on deciding to place the whole church under one sole large vault, based on the free, flexible reinterpretation of the ribbed vault, stripped geometric rigidity. But this is not just a system of vaults that counteract each other establishing the characteristic Gothic isometry, but also a hierarchical set of stepped vaults whose final outline is an exact line with the system of weight distribution for the whole roof, which runs from the top of the belfry to the floor.

But the rationality of the layout is not lacking in tauntness. On the con-

Section of the Sanctuary of Montferri, 1926 (Jujol Archive).

trary, the building finally seems to be a vibrant living organism, where each part is submitted to the limits of its capacity. It would be necessary to speak, in this case, of a kind of *agony* suffered when dealing with the architecture. Taking the meaning in its etymological sense, as a struggle of confrontation and effort.

The brilliant celebration of the harvest festival of the vineyard and wheat depicted on the murals painted in the interior are incorporated into the welcoming and dramatic image of the Sagrat Cor, an invocation which is at the same time both loving and sorrowful and which shows well the expectant suffering that the whole church exudes. It is not strange that Jujol himself, in a short text with which he presents his work in 1923, ends his explanation dedicating the efforts and difficulties of that work to another church, still to come, in which, and only in which, the final glorious resting place can be found.

Shortly after the inauguration of the church of Vistabella, Jujol received another commission of the same kind. This was also a church that was to be constructed on a small hill, some hundred metres from the town of Montferri in the Province of Tarragona. It is a sanctuary, a place to visit, set on the way from the village to the high, open space from where it overlooks the plain below.

This sanctuary would be dedicated to the Virgin of Montserrat, with all the nationalistic significance and magic which that name and place evoked in Catalunya in the mid-twenties.

In this project, Jujol tries out a different and more complex solution although having quite a few points of contact with his experience in Vistabella, and above all with the church par excellence in that cultural circle and at that time ; the church of La Sagrada Família in Barcelona. Due to its being a Sanctuary in which the access, the *promenade Architecturale* and ultimate place of worship should be joined in one sole spatial area, the project of Montferri adopts a solution which is closer to the structure of a Basilica. From the entrance door, with its welcoming gallery of funicular arches, we go into the main large aisle, lit in the centre by a pointed dome which defines the centre of this space. But following the axis which leads up to this, the Sanctuary forms a second concave space, the niche, where, at the top, the object of worship, the image of the Virgin Mary, is installed, access to which is by way of a solemnly rising flight of steps. This is the final point of the pilgrimage. Further away, thanks to a panoramic balcony, the open countryside can be seen from the top of the hill. Underneath, taking advantage of the supportive structure of the chapel housing the niche, we find an altar set deep in the rocks, thus establishing the counterpoint between the hidden cave where the image is found and the higher level where it is worshipped and consecrated. The system of ribbed vaults through the use of parabolic arches is unitary throughout the building, forming a roof of ascending arches which, as they keep rising, evoke the image of the magic mountain of Montserrat, but they are also the main reason for the organic unity of the material which is used in the structure of the roofing.

For the construction of the Sanctuary of Montferri, Jujol radicalizes to its limits his constructive layout. Only one type of material is used for the construction of the walls, arches and ornate lattice work that fills the spaces in the arches. This is a block, prefabricated *in situ*, through the use of cement and coal gangue which is used as a binding agent. Of course Jujol justified this choice of material due to the limited economic means at his disposal. But we cannot imagine that this was — in 1926 — the only reason for such a strange choice of building material. We have had occasion to see how Jujol in all his work uses poor materials — modest as we have often called them — this constitutes something more than the bad luck of always having clients of modest economic means. The modesty of his means could well be called poverty in the positive sense with which Jujol would have accepted this terminology.

Urs von Balthasar, in the studies on aesthetics carried out during the last years of his life, made a clarifying analysis on the meaning of the aesthetics of poverty in the tradition which proceeds from St Francis of Assisi: the role of Franciscanism is of greatest importance in the Gaudí circle, straddled between *Modernisme* and *Noucentisme* but wanting to be independent from both, with the aim of continuing, in the twentieth century, the Pre-Raphaelite and Nazarene experiences of the eighteen-hundreds.

It is certain that, while the splendour of the structural order searched for by Jujol and inherited from Gaudí, proceed from the rich mine of the teachings of Aristotle and Thomas transmitted to the Gaudí circle by Torres i Bages, on the other hand, in the apparently naïve, weak and poor attitude of Jujol's architecture there appears a sensitivity which is different because it is the only art that can see the infinite, precisely through what is most frail, ephemeral and poor.

5.Conclusions

Jujol's work presents itself to us as multiple and pluriform. From the elaborate ecclesiastical buildings to the most insignificant objects, the whole of his work adheres to the unity of a person who carries out his work free from conventional artistic limitations.

In a sense Jujol shows us clearly how modern he is, precisely because of the impossibility of dividing his work into separate compartments, on the other hand he and his world are far removed from what has been considered the official avant-garde history of the twentieth century, and also in that neither ideologically nor technically was his starting point that of the artists of an advanced industrial society. This is without doubt the reason why canonic history has not found him a place in the art and architecture of the XX century.

That great anomaly of which Eugeni d'Ors spoke when referring to Gaudí is also applicable in the case of Jujol; but anomaly does not mean anything other than being outside the conventional rules that define the course of art of our century from a particular hypothesis and current trends.

It is time, however, to remake lineal history and find a way of understanding the art of our century where such fascinating figures as the one we have studied here have a place and an adequate explanation.

We feel that it is naïve to try and draw sectional parallels within which it can be said that Jujol is a forerunner of *collage*, surrealism, *arte povera* or deconstructivism. These are topics which can be elaborated in essays but which instead of being clarifying are confusing.

We propose to offer a study of Jujol's case from the point of view of its own particular history and circumstances. Only from these can we gain a certain understanding of this architect.

The reader will allow us, therefore, as a final résumé, to offer a sort of decalogue to synthesize the notes of what, in our opinion, best characterises Jujol's contribution. This

Lluis Casals

Project of the monumental fountain for the International Exhibition of Barcelona, in Plaça Espanya, 1928 (Jujol Archive).

is an open-ended way of working, always in process. His work does not rise out of a finished system, nor from a precise aesthetic programme but is characterised by its exploration, by the tentative sounding out of possibilities. It is in this perspective of the artist as an explorer of the boundaries that Jujol's work takes on fascinating contemporary features.

1. The first exploration we recognise in the whole of Jujol's work is that of the boundaries between painting and architecture. If we had to re-write Laocoön, nothing would be better than to take note of this work to find numerous boundary situations. Jujol's pupils in his drawing classes always spoke of his skill of creating a form based on areas of color, a scrap of paper or a trickle of paint. With brushes or with his fingers, that accident grew, moved and took on shape on the paper of the awkward student. It is from this way of making shapes grow on paper that we are able to understand also the growth of his shapes in space, with recurrences, *ritornellos*, derivations, localised explosions.

2. For this reason architecture is at all times personalized. It is not autobiographical in the sense that it is based on the problems arising from the work in hand, but it is autobiographical in the sense of the architect who is above any type of dividing up of his work and who, instead, participates at all stages and at all levels in the construction of a building. It goes without saying that the abstract medition of plans, calculations and documents loses importance. It is the drawings, and often not even these, that bear witness to the process through which the author is involved at all times. The craft element of Jujol's architecture does not only speak of his tactile character but also bears the personal stamp of the author and shows the complete absence of separation between the author and his work.

3. Craftsmanship, without a doubt, occupies a prime position and even more so the exacerbation of converting the architect into a manual worker. The debate Craft versus Industry, so characteristic of the end of the nineteenth century, flourishes in the field of architecture. There is no doubt that the great architects of the moment, Sullivan, Berlague, Domènech i Montaner each gave their particular answers. Jujol's answer, still linked with that problem, is radical and critical. His anti-modernism — in the philosophical not the stylistic sense of the word — is total.

4. The Catholic circle in which we place Jujol in the end-of-century culture represented, from time immemorial inspired by the idealization of the Middle Ages, one of the first critical trends of modern culture. Springing from the fertile ground of Franciscanism, the criticism of the modern world is an expression of inadequateness. The option for manual work, for farming, for the exasperation of small works, the malign anticonventional, established anologies with the other strong critical trends of modern life: Dadaism and Surrealism. To speak of Jujol as a surrealist lends itself to confusion. It is obvious to discern a critical attitude and some linguistic techniques which are proper to the modern fragmentation, which are, in certain aspects, parallel to those of Surrealism. The ambiguity between criticism and reaction that we find in Jujol is of the same type that we find, for example, in Miró or Max Ernst.

5. If it is possible to speak of weak architecture in the sense of the way of working that reflects the insecurity of the contemporary culture, then this weakness can be found in Jujol. This does not refer to the personal convictions of the architect, but to the temporariness which always seems to be present in his work.

Jujol's architecture is not based on Vitrubian *firmitas*. He does not base the technology of his work on the challenge to the passing of time. Instead of an immovable presence and a permanent structure, this is a type of architecture which is temporarily encamped upon another building, in fragile urban structures, which are badly constructed, built to last only for a certain time.

6. Jujol's architecture shuns *l'esprit de systéme*. The desire to organise from the most general to the most particular details. On the contrary, it is erratic and auto-constructive, growing from unexpected movements based on casual displacements of energy.

7. The technical language of this architecture is of action carried out at specific points. Places of poetic reaction, we could say paraphrasing the famous expression by Le Corbusier. In the formation of modern consciousness, the importance of the tradition of psychology in the picturesque is very often scorned. But its effectiveness in reflecting one of the features of modern sensitivity — the temporariness of the esthetic experience — is also clear in Jujol. The fact that Jujol's work takes us from one thing to another, from one place to another, is but the reflection, in the most symptomatic sense, of the modernity of his sensitivity.

8. If in modern art each work bears its code, we can say that in the case of Jujol, his architecture does not have a code with which to understand it but does have a permanent decoding mechanism as a vehicle of expression. It works like a meta-language of previously known codes — stylistic, of ordinary daily images, of great architecture — caught up in the process of linguistic collision. More than being the formulation of a code for deciphering the work, this consists of the interrelation of many codes in a process of juxtapositioning and conflict, which is characteristic of all currents of criticism.

9. Introducing the concept of time in a work is a typically modern operation. This can be produced in two ways: by spatial diversification or by the mark of the process. We have already mentioned spatial diversification as a policentric and uncoor-

dinated technique of intervention. No less important, however, are the signs of the process of the work. Jujol's buildings all seem to be unfinished, but this is not only because in all of them there is no end. The work is a process and is shown as such, always open to new interventions. It displays the point which the work being carried out had reached at that moment.

10. Jujol is often spoken of as a great architect who never had the right kind of clients. In other words, as an architect he had to supply with his genius what was lacking in the economic conditions of his work. I believe that this is deceiving. His is a type of architecture which is rich, luxurious, sensual and exuberant despite the poverty of its materials and means. The fascination of Jujol's architecture lies however in this paradox: his having created a limited universe which is rich and fascinating, but without having to resort to the commonplaces of what is normally considered to be the richness and abundance of architecture.

Lourdes Jansana

Altar of Sant Josep for the crypt of the Colònia Güell, Santa Coloma de Cervelló (Barcelona), 1943 (Jujol Archive).

Chronological Summary*

1879 Josep M.ª Jujol is born in Tarragona.

1902 Design of sgraffiti and railings for La Casa Gallissà (collaboration with Antoni M.ª Gallissà), Barcelona.

1904 The reforming of the Barcelona Ateneo (collaboration with Josep M.ª Font Gumà) Barcelona.
Project in the School of Architecture: Historical Archive of Catalunya.

1905 Project in the School of Architecture: Votive church dedicated to Santa Eulàlia.

1906 End of career project: Thermal Baths building. Design of Casa Batlló (collaboration with Antoni Gaudí). Barcelona.

1907 Design in the Casa Milà (collaboration with Antoni Gaudí) Barcelona.

1908 Paintings in the old city walls (scattered work, commissioned by Gaudí). Carrer Tapineria, Barcelona. Workers' Association Theater, Tarragona.

1909 Torre San Salvador, Barcelona.

1910 Ornamentation of some street lights for the Commemoration of the Centenary of Jaume Balmes (collaboration with Antoni Gaudí), Vic (Barcelona).
Project for a Standard for the Cercle Artístic Sant Lluc (artistic circle).
Design of elements and paintings for the restoration of the Cathedral of Palma (collaboration with Antoni Gaudí).

1911 Design of elements for the Park Güell (collaboration with Antoni Gaudí). The Manyac shop (Barcelona).

1913 Design of the lift for the Casa Iglesias, Barcelona.
Torre de la Creu. Sant Joan Despí (Barcelona).

1914 Casa Ximenis, Tarragona.
Renovation of the Mas Bofarull, Els Pallaresos (Tarragona).

1915 "Radial" water fountain, Barcelona.
Restoration of the Casa Negre, Sant Joan Despí (Barcelona).

1916 The Manyac factory, Barcelona.

1917 Torre Queralt, Barcelona.
School and Town Council building, Els Pallaresos (Tarragona).
The finish of the belltower of the church of Creixell de Mar (Tarragona).
Design of a tombstone for the Planelles family Cementiri Nou in Montjuïc, Barcelona.

* This chronology is a summary of the most complete one published to date of the work: Josep M.ª Jujol, Arquitecto 1879-1949. Un catálogo razonado, "Quaderns d'Arquitectura i Urbanisme" (Barcelona), 1989.

1918-1923 Church of Vistabella (Tarragona).

1919 Niche del Carme. Carmelite Church, Tarragona.
Design of a tombstone for the Sant Salvador family Cementiri Nou in Montjuïc, Barcelona.

1920-1923 Renovation of the Casa Fortuny, Els Pallaresos, Tarragona.

1921-1927 One family house: Casa Serra Xaus Sant Joan Despí (Barcelona).

1923 Block of dwellings: Casa Planelles. Av. Diagonal 332, Barcelona.
Drawing of embroidery motifs on a cushion for his fiancée.
Project for the public library in Barcelona (contest organised by the Mancomunitat).

1924 Project for a one family house. Casa Jujol. Sant Joan Despí (Barcelona).
One family house: Casa Canalias. Sant Joan Despí, (Barcelona).
One family house: Casa Xaus Amigó, Sant Joan Despí (Barcelona).

1925 Design of a tombstone for the Guinovart family. Municipal Cemetery, Tarragona.

1926 Project for town planning in the neighbourhood of Samontà, Sant Joan Despí (Barcelona).
Remodeling of the chapel of Sant Francesc, Rambla de Sant Carles Baixada de Sant Francesc, Tarragona.
Development project for the Roman Amphitheatre in Tarragona.
Church sanctuary of Montferri, Montferri (Tarragona).
Design of a fountain for the Sanctuary of Nostra Senyora de Loreto. Brafim (Tarragona).
Remodeling of the Hermitage of Nostra Senyora de Loreto. Renau, (Tarragona).

1927 Jujol marries Teresa Gibert.
Remodeling of the Hermitage of Roser. (Tarragona).
Designs for his own household furniture.
Renovation of a Masia (Farmhouse): Casa Po-Cardona, Sant Joan Despí (Barcelona).
Design of a window grille: Casa Solé. Els Pallaresos (Tarragona).
Palacio del Vestido (Pavilion for the Universal Exhibition, in collaboration with Andrés Calzada), Barcelona.

1928 Torre Camprubí, Sant Joan Despí (Barcelona).
Memorial fountain for the Universal Exhibition, Plaça d'Espanya, Barcelona.

1929 Renovation of a house: Casa Claramunt. Sant Joan Despí (Barcelona).

1930 Designs for tombstones for the Arana family. Municipal Cemetery, Tarragona.
Design for the Processional float of the Holy Sepulchre for the Gremi de Pagesos (Farmer's association) of the Church of Sant Llorenç (Tarragona).

1931-1943 Renovation and design of elements in the Church of Vendrell. El Vendrell (Tarragona).

1932 Casa Jujol, Sant Joan Despí (Barcelona).
Casa Passani. Sant Joan Despí (Barcelona).

1933 Casa Casas, Sant Joan Despí (Barcelona).

1934 Renovation and design of elements for the church of Roda de Berà (Tarragona).

1935 Decorating in the Mas Carreras. Roda de Berà (Tarragona).

1939 Project of the Presbytery for the Sanctuary of Nostra Senyora de Loreto in Brafim (Tarragona).

1940 Reforming of the lecture hall and work archive of the School of Architecture in the Universitat Central Barcelona.
Project for the "Porta Heroica" for the School of Architecture.
Design of the Presbytery and altar of the Church of Guimerà (Lleida).
Reforming of the Church of Sant Llorenç and elements for the Gremi de Pagesos, Tarragona.

1939-1940 Project for the renovation of the interior of the Convent of Santa Mónica, Barcelona.

1941-1944 Restoration and design of elements in the Masia de Bonastre (Tarragona).

1942 Reconstruction of the Rose window and project for the high altar for the Basílica del Pi. Plaça del Pi, Barcelona.
Design for a memorial stone of Santa Joaquima de Vedruna in the Basílica del Pi. Plaça del Pi, Barcelona.

1943 Decoration of the interior of the Church of Sant Joan Despí (Barcelona).

1943-1948 Design for the altar for the chapel of the Colònia Güell. Santa Coloma de Cervelló (Barcelona).
Refurbishing of the Torre Codina in the neighbourhood of Canyet, Badalona (Barcelona).

1944 Alterations to and decoration of the Chapel of Mas Carreras, Roda de Berà (Tarragona).

1945-1947 Design of altars for the Church of Els Pallaresos (Tarragona).

1947 Design of high altar and presbytery for the Casa del Amparo de Vilanova i la Geltrú (Barcelona).

1947-1948 Design of stained glass windows and altar for the Parish Church of Sant Antoni, Vilanova i la Geltrú (Barcelona).

1948 Reforms to the Parish Church of Santa Coloma de Gramenet (Barcelona).

1949 Josep M.ª Jujol dies in Barcelona.

Bibliography

J.F. RÀFOLS. "Jujol," *Cuadernos de Arquitectura* (Barcelona), 3rd trimester, 1950.

CARLOS FLORES. "Algunas precisiones en torno a la obra de J.M. Jujol," *Hogar y Arquitectura*, no. 101, 1972.

J.F. RÀFOLS, CARLOS FLORES, SALVADOR TARRAGÓ, J.M.ª JUJOL (son). *La arquitectura de J.M.ª Jujol*, Barcelona: COAC, 1974.

RAFAEL MONEO. "Jujol Siza: Arquitectura en los márgenes," *Arquitecturas Bis*, no. 2, March, 1976.

ORIOL BOHIGAS. "Josep M.ª Jujol," *Arquitectura Bis*, no. 12, March-September, 1976.

MOLENAAR. "Jujol, een inspirerend vakman," *Technisches* (Delft), 1977.

PAUL DE VROOM. "De invloed van Jujol op Gaudí," *Technisches*, (Delft), 1979.

CARLOS FLORES. *Gaudí, Jujol y Modernismo Catalán*, Madrid: Ed. Aguilar, 1982.

VARIUS AUTHORS. "An Introduction and Guide to the Architecture of Jujol," *Sites* (New York), no. 8/9, 1983.

J.A. LLINÀS. "Josep M.ª Jujol, architectus: 1879-1949," *Quaderns d'Arquitectura i Urbanisme*, November-December, 1984.

JOSEP M.ª JUJOL (son). "Jujol at Park Güell," *Sites*, no. 15, 1986.

RONALD CHRIST. "Reading Jujol's inscriptions at Park Güell," *Sites*, no. 15, 1986.

PERE CASAJOANA. *La Fontana de la Plaza de España*. Doctoral Thesis. ETSAB, 1986 (unpublished).

MANUEL GAUSA. "Delirio y razón: el diseño en Jujol," *Quaderns d'Architectura i Urbanisme*, no. 174, July-September, 1987.

MONTSERRAT DURAN ALBAREDA. *Jujol a Sant Joan Despí, 1913-1949*, Barcelona: Ed. CMB, 1988.

PEREJAUME. *Ludwig Jujol*, Barcelona: Cotlliure, ed. de la Magrana, 1989.

VARIOUS AUTHORS. "Josep M.ª Jujol, Arquitecto 1879-1949. Un catálogo razonado," *Quaderns d'Arquitectura i Urbanisme* (Barcelona), no. 179-180, 1989.

Josep M.ª Jujol around 1927 (Jujol Archive).

Casa Gallissà

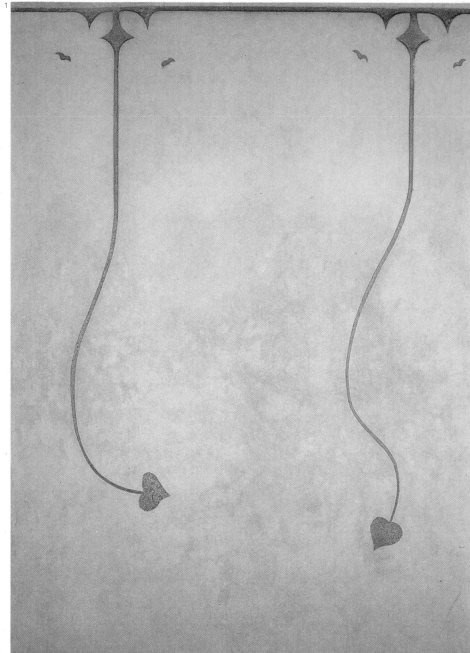

1.Detail of the sgraffiti ornamentation.
2.Figure and support of ceramics.
3.Hall.

Casa Batlló

Casa Milà "La Pedrera"

6,7,8,9. Wrought-iron balustrade on the main façade.
10,12. Ornamentation in the main hall (vestibule).
11. Detail of the hall and wrought-iron gate.

Park Güell

13,14,15,16,17,18. Details of continuous bench in the main square.
19,20. Signs and anagrams on the ceramic tops, crests.

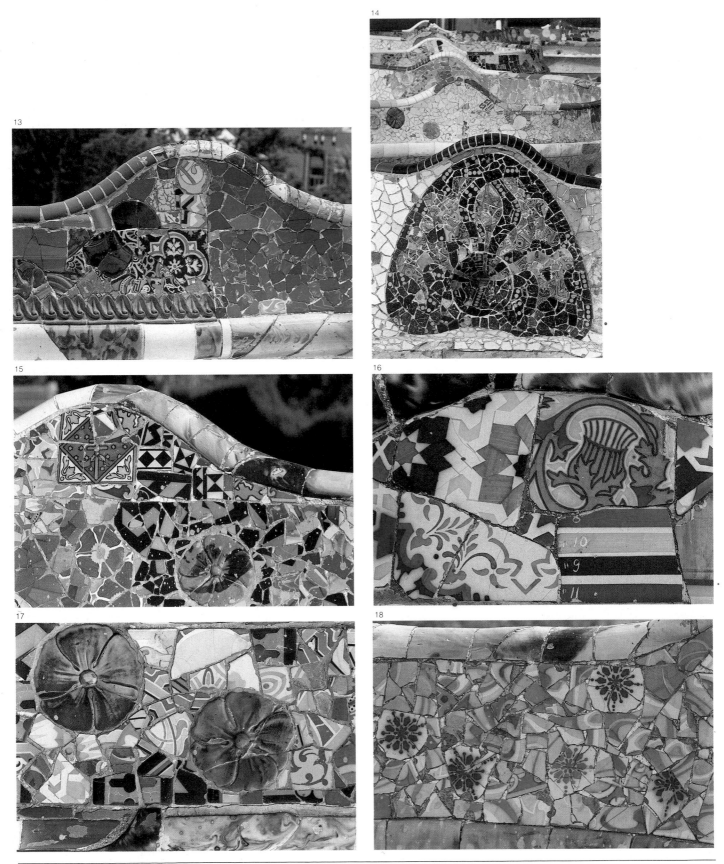

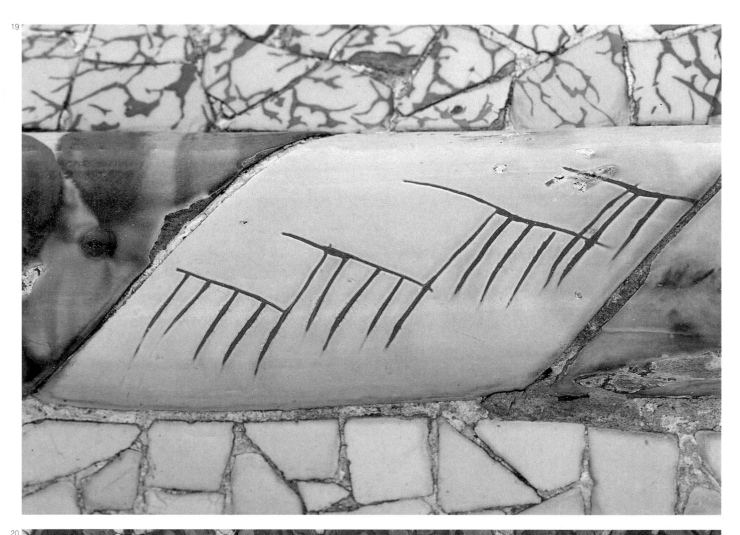

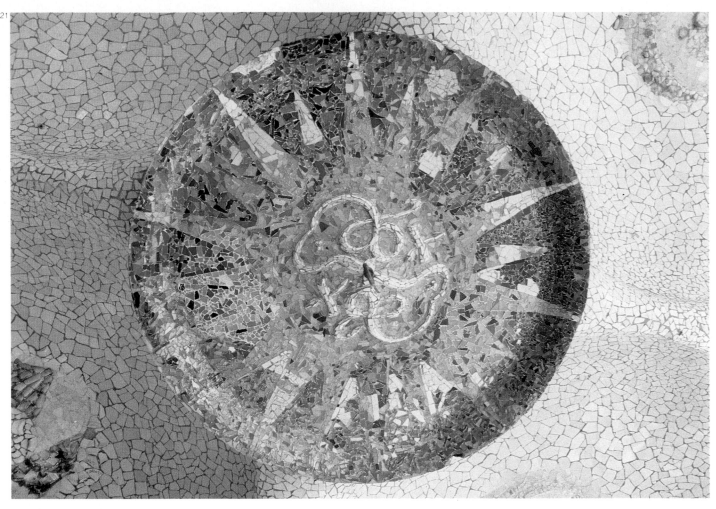

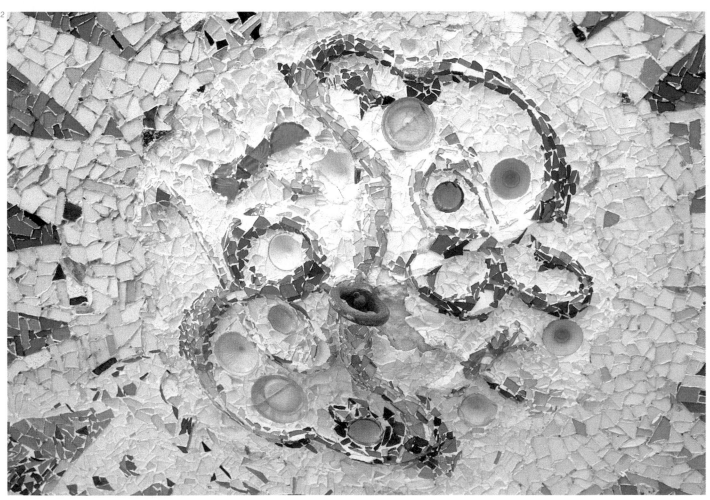

21,22,23,24,25,26. Ornamental ceramic and glass medallions in the domes of the hypostyle hall.

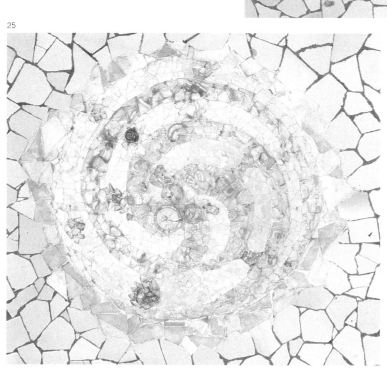

The Cathedral of Mallorca

27. Canopy above high altar.
28. Canopy lamps.
29. Ornamentation of canopy.

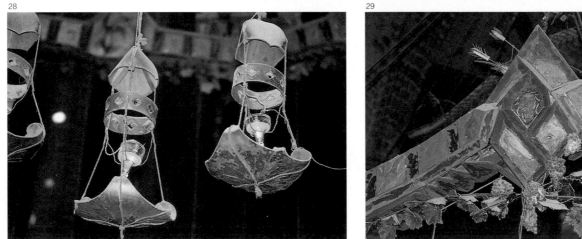

30,31,32. Ornamentation above
the choir stalls.
33. Folding foot-stools.

The Workers' Association
Theater of Tarragona

34. Ornamental brazier originally
situated on the roof.
35,36. Exterior adornment.

37,38. Details of ceiling and railing
of the dress circle.
39. Railings of the main flight of steps.
40. Detail of the window.

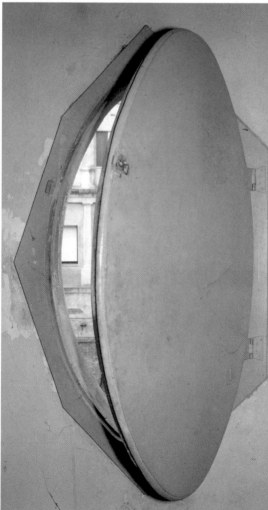

Parish Church of Constantí

41,42. Benches of carved wood.
43,44. Ornamental panels in carved wood.
45,46,47,48. Detail of wrought-iron railings of the high altar.

Casa Iglesias

49. Metal protection enclosing the lift shaft.
50. Lift of curved wood.

Casa de la Creu

51. General view.
52. Detail of the lock of the main iron-gate.
53. Roofs.

54,55,56. Details of the ornamentation and roof grids.

57. Circular balcony on the ground floor.
58. Lower part of the living-rooms.
59,60,61,62. Details of parts of the roof.

63,64,65,67. Spiral staircase leading from the ground floor to the upper floors.
66. Detail of the spiral staircase leading to the roofs.

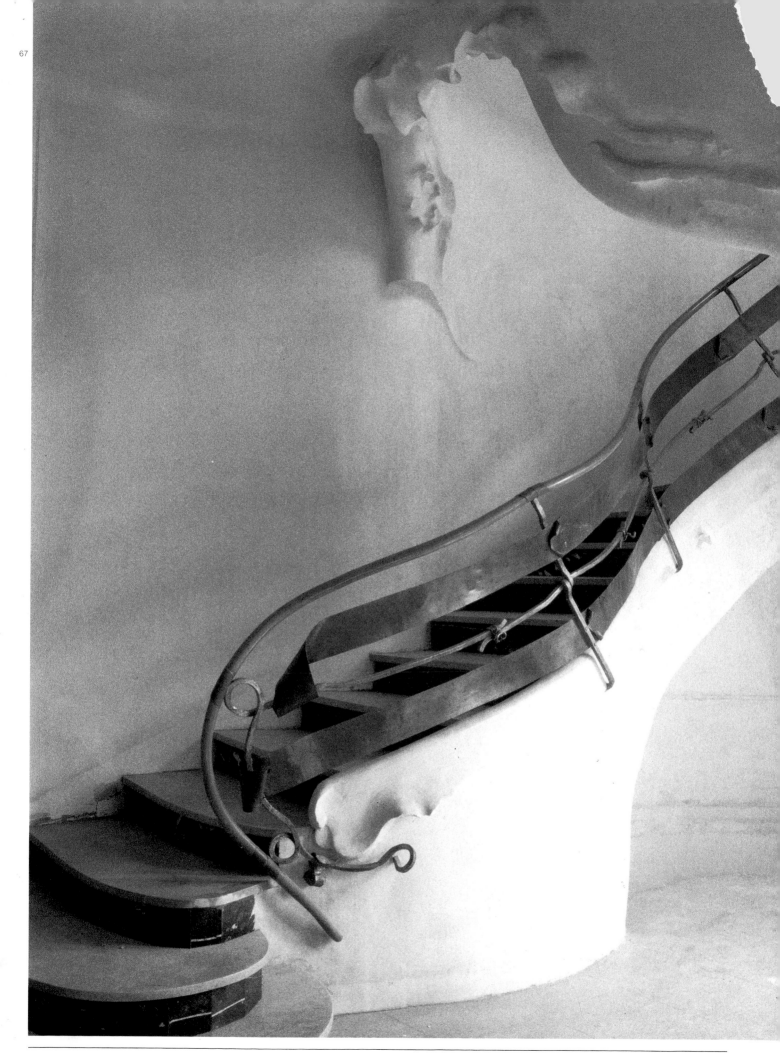

Casa Bofarull

68,70. View facing the west from the new gallery.
69. Detail of the turret.

68

69

70

72

73

71. Large triangular window set in the
garden wall.
72,73. Details of the turret.

74

74. Door-knocker and woodwork of main door.
75,76. Façade of annexe. Detail.
77,78,79. Wash-house. Details of the arcades of the pergola, door and window.

75

76

77

78

79

80,81,82,83,84,85. Main door. Details of ironwork.

86,87. Garden facing the west. Large window set in the garden wall and fountain.

Casa Negre

88

92,93,94,95. Details of sgraffiti, wrought-iron work and woodwork on the main façade.

96,97. Wrought-iron gate in the side alley. Details.
98. Adornment in the garden.
99,100. Details of sgraffiti.
101. Garden wall.

102,103. Table and bench covered with ceramics in the garden.

104. Main stairway.
105. Ornamentation of the first-floor door.
106. Vault in the main stairway.

107,108,109,110.Details of the vault above
the main stairs.
111.Exterior of the lantern in the vault of
the main stairs.

112,113,114,115. Chapel. Altar and details of the ornamentation.

112

113

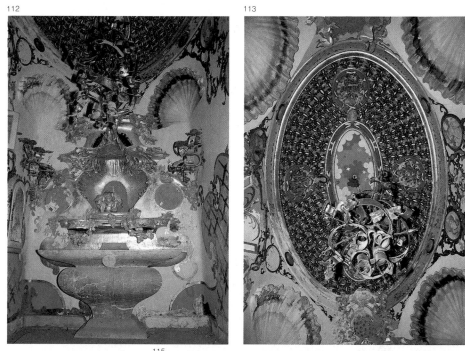

114

115

116,117,120,121,122. Chapel.
Details of the adornment.
118,119. Details of the door leading
to the chapel.

121

120

122

Torre Queralt

123

Parish Church of Creixell

128.Bell tower with the parabolic cupola.
129.Detail of the cupola and the parabolic arches.

Church of Vistabella

131. Detail of the porch.
132. Triangular spire and bell tower.
133. View of the whole church from the main porch.

132

133

134,135,136,137,138. Details of the exterior roof.

136

138

137

139,140,141,142. Details of the arcades with the choir balustrade.
143.A series of arches in one of the side chapels.

144,145,146,147. Details of the interior pictorial ornamentation.

148. Candelabra.
149. Baptismal font.
150,151. Side altars.

149

148

150

151

Casa Fortuny (Ca l'Andreu)

152

152,154. Detail of the main entrance.
153. Main façade.
155. Vestibule flooring.

153

154

155

156,158,160,161. Vestibule. Details.
157,159. Dining-room. Window and
cupboard.

Tallers Manyac

162

162,163,164. Skylights, buttresses and domes.

164

163

Casa Bruguera

168

169. Detail of the grating.
170. Detail of the first floor gallery.

171. Main stairway and entrance door.
172,173. Detail of the main flight of steps.

179,180,181. Ornamentation main façade. Details.

179

180

171. Main stairway and entrance door.
172,173. Detail of the main flight of steps.

172

173

174,175. Details of the main stairway.
176,177,178. Lounge on the first floor.
Details.

174

175

176

177

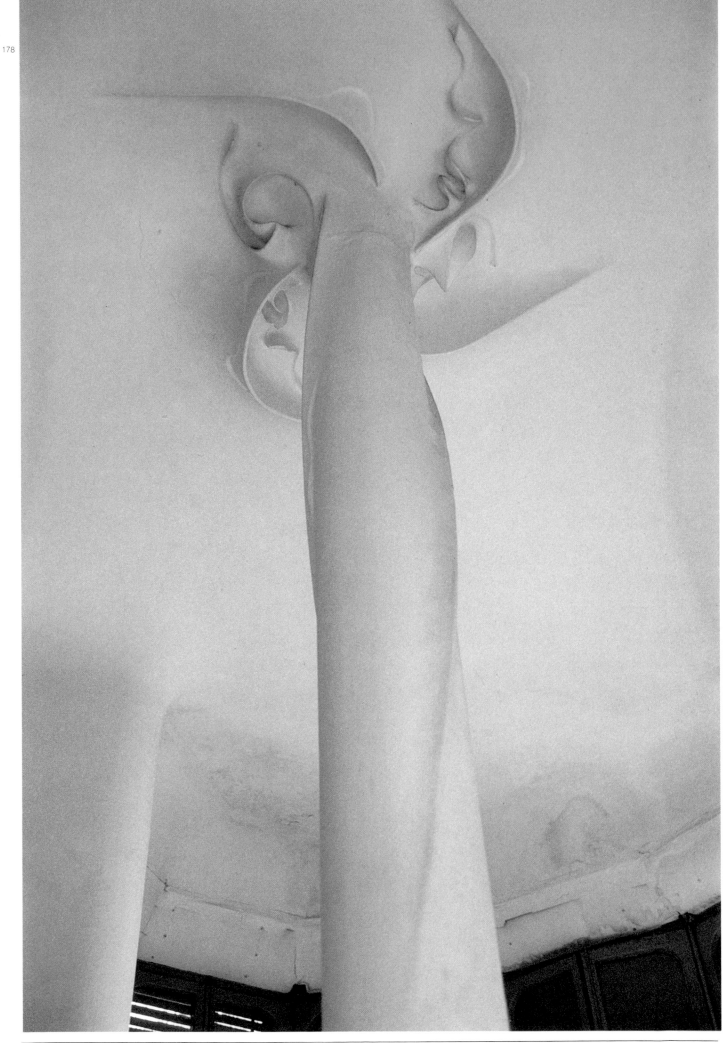

182,183,184,185,186. Ornamental sgraffiti on the interior walls.

183

184

187

188

187,188,189,190,191,192. Details of flooring.

189

190

191

192

193.Detail of flooring.
194.Ornamentation of the large window.
195.Interior of the main door.
196.Lampholder of wrought-iron.

Hermitage of Renau

197,198. Main façade. Detail.

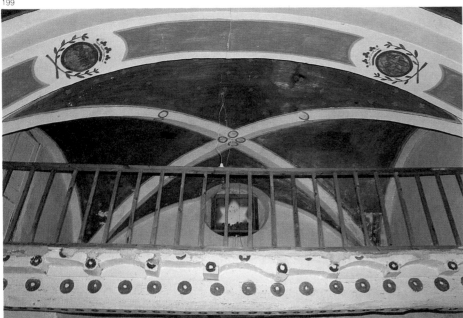

199

200

202

201

199,100,201,202. Ornamentation in the choir of the nave of the chapel.

Sanctuary of Montferri

203. Exterior structure for the small niche and the chapel in the cavern.
204. Lateral façade.

205. Main aisle. View of the
entrance porch.
206. Detail of the structure
of the arches.

207. Lateral façade.
208. Dome above the high altar.
209. Detail of the lattice covering of the large windows.

207

208

210,211,212. Arches of the aisles.

213. The Sanctuary at the top of the hill.
214. Enclosure wall of reinforced concrete with wire netting.
215. Portal dome.
216. Main dome.
217,218,220. Details of the arches.
219. Access to the dressing-room and the sacristy.

213

214

215

216

Casa Rovira

221,222,223.Details of the sgraffiti on the main façade.

Casa Cebrià

224. Details of the large windows set in angle.
225. Detail of the sgraffiti.
226. View of the building.

Fountain in the Plaça d'Espanya

227. Detail of the balustrade and the fountain.
228. Main tower of the fountain.
229. Medallion in bas-relief.

Casa Jujol

230. Detail of the wooden grille.
231. Ornamentation of the window.
232. Detail of the entrance door.

Casa Serra-Xaus

233. Detail of the roofs.
234. Sgraffiti.
235. Detail of the entrance porch.

Parish Church of
Els Pallaresos

236. Ornamention and stained-glass in a side window.
237. Detail of the pedestal.
238. Detail of the collection box.

Parish Church of
Sant Joan Despí

239.Detail of the pulpit.
240.Detail of the wooden benches.
241.High altar and monstrance.

Parish Church of Bonastre

242.Baptismal font.
243.Monstrance.

The Church of
Sant Francesc

244,245. Ornamentation above
the lateral arches.
246. Vaulted niche decorated
with sgraffiti.

Casa de l'Empar

247. Monstrance.
248. Ornamental detail.
249. High altar.

Parish Church of Guimerà

250. Detail of the High Altar.
251. Monstrance.
252. Pedestal.
253. High Altar.

Index of illustrations